COMPUTER
LESSONS
FOR THE BEGINNERS
OF ALL AGES

****

STEP-BY-STEP INSTRUCTIONS

E-MAIL, INTERNET, BROWSING

CHATTING, AND GAMES

COMPUTER LANGUAGE

PHOTO ILLUSTRATIONS

CONNECTING TO THE SERVER

IF THEY NEED HELP

TELEPHONE, FAX, EMAIL.

IF YOU HAVE FOUND OTHER COMPUTER
HOW-TO BOOKS UNSUCCESFUL,
PLEASE TURN THE PAGE FOR
A NICE SURPRISE

DUSTY RHOADS

OUR CONFIDENT OFFER

If you have read this book in sequence, have picked out any lesson, and, after following the directions carefully, you have not been successful, call us. Within twelve days of our mailing, Return the book, and your money will be returned.

To order additional copies of this book, contact:
Xlibris Corporation
1-888-795-4274
www.Xlibris.com
Orders@Xlibris.com
47583

CONTENTS

WHAT IS THE INTENTION OF THIS BOOK?

To enable beginners to enjoy the purchase of their computer, or those who are contemplating the purchase of a computer, or to relieve the minds of many that we believe are interested in a computer but, to date, have been turned off by the technical jargon that has spread throughout the computer world, causing many to say, Oh, I could never learn to use one of those things.

We know, however, that they can and, with a degree of enlightenment, end the frustration of many, saving the expense of replacing a great deal of window glass smashed with a computer, leaving the premises by the fastest and shortest route into orbit—this should never happen if you follow this guide as your guide to enjoyable fun.

I have taken pains to make sure I am using understandable language and step-by-step guidelines to avoid stubbing your toe or having to run to the bookstore to purchase a book for nitwits or on what every idiot should know about the Internet. I do not consider my readers to be idiots or dummies; I do assume they have spent little or no time sitting in front of a computer monitor, keyboard, or tower (computer case).

Now let us briefly say a little about how it all began. The people that developed the computer, World Wide Web (www), Internet, etc.—the intelligent wizards—said to themselves, Hey! We have something going here, and we had better do something about it or the first thing you know, everyone will want to get in on the act. What should we wizards do? Well, first, let's create our own language, and if someone is standing around listening, we can throw in a little Latin. Then instead of a new language, let's use some English, but we can mix it up a bit so when we are talking, or even writing and mentioning download or hard drive or other delightful words, they will never have any idea what we are talking about.

Unfortunately, we were not around to stop this miscarriage of intelligence before it got started. Now, however, we are in a position to explain what they had in mind, so take heart. And please don't give up, for in a very short time, as you proceed to finish this book, I will have you well versed in the language, and I will do it in half the space and time of the gurus.

As you go through the book and the table of contents, if you do not find the lesson that interest you, you may find it has not been included. Sorry. Please remember, you are still beginning, and what is being provided will help you to answer many questions on your own. If not, you are very welcome to contact me by phone or to turn to the section for sending e-mail. If I do not have the information you need, I will know where to get it, and all you have to do is tell me how and where you want the information returned to you.

A FEW WORDS AND DEFINITIONS THAT MAY HELP IN THE BEGINNING

ATTACH   Take a file and attach it to an e-mail and send it.

BYTE   A measure of storage.

BOOKMARK   Place you want to return to on the Internet.

BROWSER   A unit you can use to locate pages on the World Wide Web.

BUTTON   An electric switch called a button.

CD-ROM   Memory held on a CD.

CHATTING   To talk to others on the Internet through typing.

CONNECT   When you have Internet or other computers connected.

CURSOR   A blinking dash where you can start to type. The mouse arrow is sometimes called a cursor.

CTRL   A special key on the keyboard for advanced commands.

CUT   To remove text or art and place or paste it in a new position.

DEFAULT   The action taken when the computer does not receive a command or does not need one.

DESKTOP   Your monitor screen, showing the icons of programs and files.

DRIVERS   The units that control CDs, floppies, and some programs.

FLOPPY   A unit in which to store or file text from the computer.

FORMATTING   Preparing either a floppy or a disk for a particular job or system.

HARD DRIVE   A unit or device that contains the hard disc.

HISTORY   A record of places you have visited on the Internet.

HTTP (hypertext transfer protocol)
         Used to transfer Web pages over the Internet.

ENCRYPTION   To scramble code or password to protect information.

ISP (Internet service provider)
         Acronym for Internet service provider.

INTERNET   A network to allow communication all over the world through e-mail or chatting (www).

LINK   To place the arrow on a page to get to another page.

LOG OFF   To disconnect from the server.

LOG ON   To connect with your server.

MAXIMIZE   To enlarge an image to its largest capacity.

MENU   A list of options inside a program.

MICROSOFT INTERNET EXPLORER/NESCAPE NAVIGATOR
         Two of the largest Internet programs.

MODEM   Used to communicate to computers by telephone lines.

MOUSE   A device to move the arrow on the screen at your direction.

OPEN   To activate or look into a folder file or program.

PASTE   To insert copy or art previously cut or copied from the original work.

PHONE   Using your modem to connect to a computer.

POT (not what you think)
                            This is a device most gurus have forgotten how to use, a plain old telephone.

SEARCH ENGINE   A unit designed to find information on the net.

SOFTWARE   A type of computer program intended to get the hardware moving.

TAGS   Electric buttons named to make individual selections.

TILE OR TILING   Arranging windows in like sizes, in order, and not overlapping.

URL (uniform resource locator)
                            A page or address on the net.

WEB   Is www on Internet.

WINDOW   The screen, a segment of the screen, a framed area inside a procedure. You and I might call it an insert.

PHOTOS OF COMPONENTS

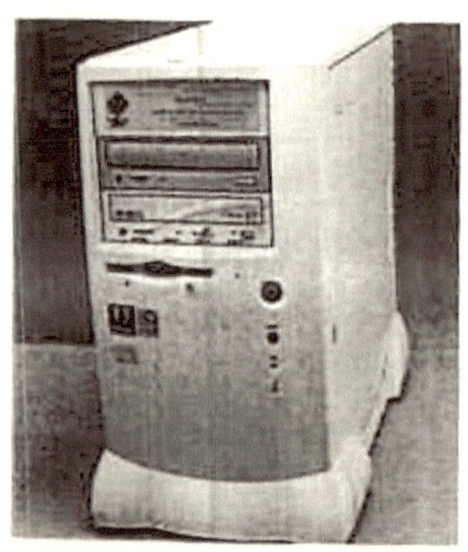

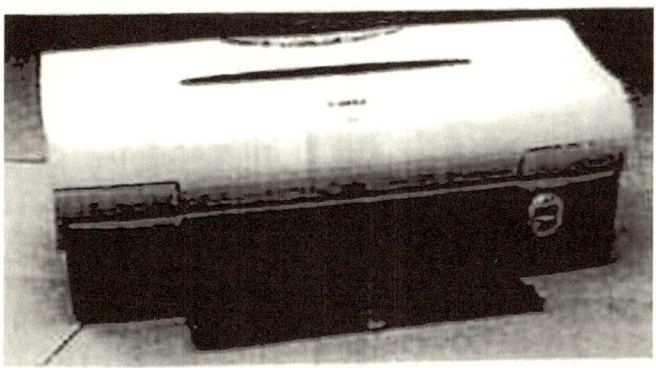

WIRING DIAGRAM

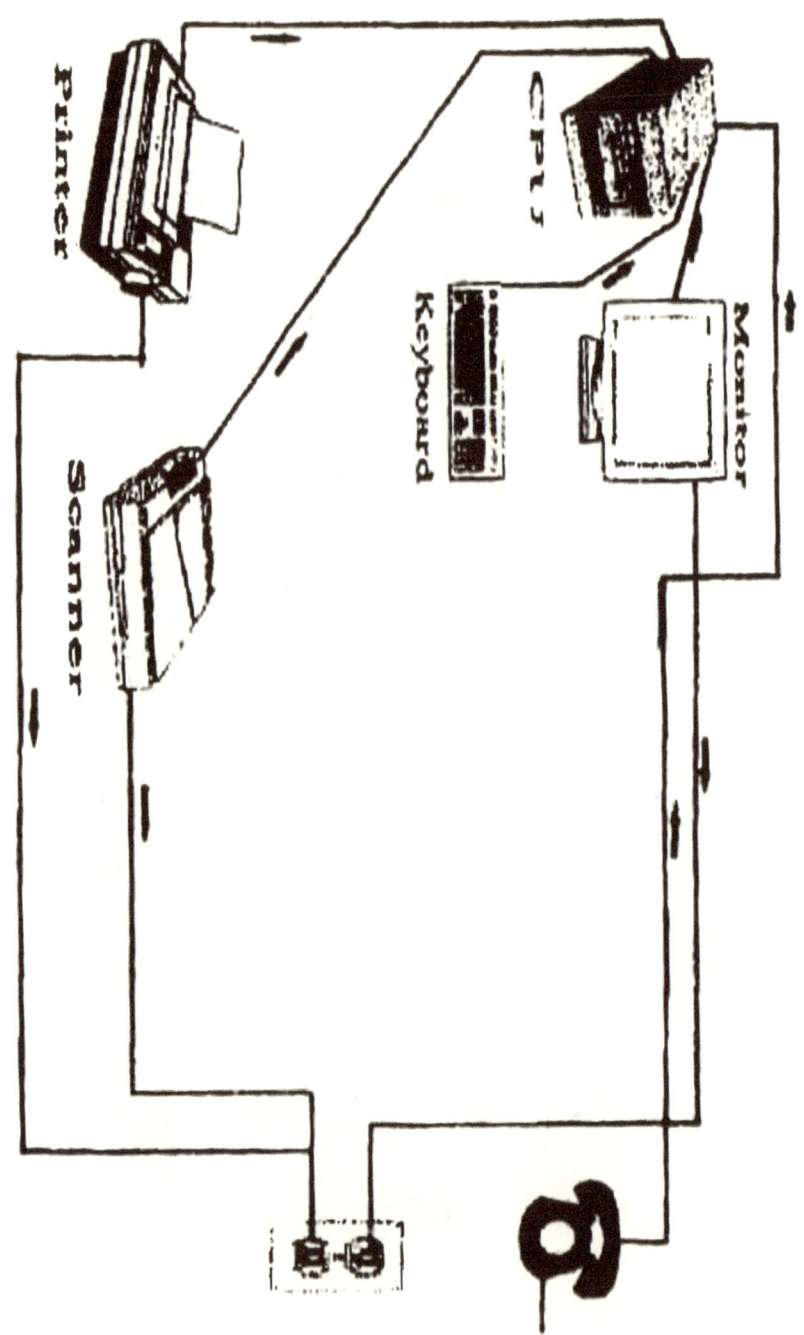

CONNECTING UP WIRES AND CABLES

How to and what to buy. If you are buying from out of the country or in Mexico, keep in mind the language unless you are bilingual. Don't shy away from Mexico or any other foreign manufacturers; many computer components are universal.

Now that we have the units, how do we handle all the wires and cables? First of all, the cables and wires have a built-in code in the way they are made. Shape, size, number of prongs, etc., make it nearly impossible to put the cable in the wrong socket (depending on how strong you are), and you don't have to know where the wire will go. Just keep trying carefully till you find the right plug or socket that fits. Now look over every item, and make sure all units that have On/Off switches are turned to Off. Take a deep breath, pick up the 110-volt power cords and plug them into the 110-volt sockets.

That's right, nothing blew up. Of course not. Now turn on each unit one at a time and nothing blows up as well. Now let's throw in a few suggestions. Buy six inlet sockets with a single 110-volt plug and plug this into a power surge guard. If you don't have one, pick one up from where you bought your equipment. This way you can turn things on and off one at a time. Check the wiring diagram, it will give you a basic idea of the required cable layout. When everything is working and in fine shape, I suggest that you identify all your plugs and sockets. If and when you may have to disconnect, you can do it with ease. I know, I have been there.

We won't let this happen to you.

CONNECTING WITH AN INTERNET SERVICE PROVIDER

This procedure, along with the questions involved, is rather difficult for one not living in your area. If you live in Mexico, you can contact Telnor, the Mexican national phone system, and they can connect you while you are on the phone. Should you feel that you do not want to be limited in this new game you are about play, then you will need or want a telephone line, or perhaps two lines if the computer is to be located in your home. I do not want to get ahead of ourselves, but the problem is how much you intend to use the computer and, in turn, how much time you want to spend on the Internet. When you are on the Internet with one line, you will not be able to receive incoming calls.

What this means is you are probably answering your question right now. If you are willing to take this limitation and schedule around it, so be it. Many folks do. In the beginning, it is probably best to give just one line a try, at least until you have had time to study through this book and found how much fun you are going to have. You may be so delighted you will need two lines right away. Who knows?

Now about the word *modem.* This is used to refer to the device that all you need to know is how to spell it and how to connect it between the computer and the Internet service provider. Thank heavens we are just beginning; otherwise, we would have to call in an ISP, and in that case, we would have to run down the hall for the dictionary.

You think you could find ISP in your big book? ISP, Internet service provider. Well, this is the way some gurus get their kicks, but we cut them off at the pass by including some of these weird words as we go along or in our list of words that might confuse, and that covers some of the language they have messed up.

UNDERSTANDING OUR INSTRUCTIONS

Directions are beginning with the movement of the mouse arrow, which include the click on the left or the right side of the mouse and how many times to click.

When asked to go to a name on the screen, for instance Microsoft Publisher, it means, go to the Microsoft Publisher icon on the desktop and click twice. All icons require a double click; for example, when the directions are to go to spell check and click and if the number of clicks is not indicated, it means only one click. For some programs, you will be asked to click once on the left and once on the right.

Here are a few directions that you may be given for the arrow: (1) Go with the arrow to . . . (2) Take the arrow to . . . (3) Move the arrow to . . . (4) Arrow to . . . and click twice. Always click left unless right is specified. As you can see, these directions mean the same thing.

When giving directions, only plain English is used. If computer jargon must be used, it will be explained at the time in order to avoid confusion. Every attempt has been made to keep information as simple as possible. For instance, you will not read "Click once on the left side of the mouse." I will use one of the four mentioned above. Rather like not having to watch your feet while dancing. Some directions may seem a little redundant, and if you find it so, *it is intended* to avoid directions requiring you to remember or "For more information, check pages so and so"

Since we are not getting paid by the hour, I will take the risk of boring you by repeating many times the instructions of a procedure. For example, take the arrow to File on the upper bar and to the left, click it. Now a menu will appear with options to select from. I tell you what option to select by a click, and continue until the procedure is completed. You will find that File is in bold type. This will be the case when you are directed to go to a specific spot, button, tag, or menu selection.

When I say place the arrow at the beginning of your text and drag across the top line, I want you to know what dragging is before you are ever required to use it.

Of course, if you have cheated just a smidgen and did not accept my recommendation that you take each lesson in order, step-by-step, through the lesson book. Well, in that case, you will have picked up fifteen demerits and probably spoiled your weekend.

PUNCTUATION

; ? ( ) =

When you look through the book, you will find the text has been divided into four, five, or six lines, rather paragraphs, so you do not have to search through long passages to find where you left off before your break.

TO START

Everything up to this point is just fine; wires and cables are connected. The equipment is all in place. And the mouse is ready to go.

All the power is off, and if you are fortunate enough to have a power surge and low power control, great. Plug the control into the 110-volt sockets; it will have a number of receptive sockets for you to plug in all your equipment. If you do not have a surge control, your next move is to buy six or seven outlet extensions and plug in as follows: Plug in the tower, press the largest button on the tower. Next, we go to the monitor and see if there is a small light on the lower border of the monitor frame, and if so, all is well, and if you are unable to see the light hit the big button, which should be close to the little light, the big button is an On and Off switch and now the little light should be on.

You will now move the arrow directed by the mouse to the lower left-hand corner of the monitor screen, and you will find the word Start. Click on it.

I can sum up the rest of your equipment by mentioning each piece like a printer, scanner, or perhaps some digital camera equipment. These will all come with well-written instructions, to be followed carefully.

SHUTTING DOWN

This is quite simple; it is a good idea to close all the folders and programs you have been using. The upper right-hand corner of the screen should take care of it with a few clicks on X. This will leave you with the desktop.

Now with the mouse, go to Start and click it, and just above Start, click on Shut Down, and a small window will appear, giving you three choices. Pick Shut Down.

This process should be followed at all times in order to avoid irritating any wizard who may be snooping around inside your tower.

DESKTOP EXPLANATION

1   The desktop is the center of everything involved with the computer.

2   With the power on, press the large button on the tower and wait for the desktop to come on the monitor screen. After you have worked a little and made a few folders and placed a few icons, the screen will begin to look quite interesting. The lessons you are about to study will teach you how, why, and when the icons should be made and placed on the desktop. Each folder and icon will be given a name specified by you. When you are ready to refer to or call on them, it will require two left clicks.

3   One icon you will want to know about is My Computer. This is, in my opinion, a terrible name as it adds to the confusion, which is inherent in the computer world. If I should say, go to My Computer, you will at once want to know where I keep it. If you are talking to a friend, he may ask you to go to My Computer, but I do not want you to go to my computer, and he says go to My Computer on your computer. Well, if Abbot and Costello were still alive, we could make a whole sitcom out of this,

4   Along the title bar, the top of the screen on Microsoft Word, and to the far right corner, are three little squares, the first one with a dash, the second one is a little computer, and the third one is an X, which you can hit if you want to go back to your desktop, thus ending what you have been working on. The dash will minimize the window, and the middle one will maximize it.

5   Going to the bottom of the screen, you will find the taskbar. You will find on the left Start and on the opposite end is the time of day. I will

give you more information on both of these and the rest of the bars when they become important.

As you go through this little book, you will find that I have suggested clicking on buttons, folders, icons, or anything looking suspicious. It is a good way to find out what is going on. My definition of playing around is simple: you look at a button, a little symbol, one word or, perhaps six in a row, what now, who knows? Just play with them all. Try to keep track, and if possible, keep a pen handy for you might find something terrific and want to go back to it.

According to recent polls taken, no one has ever reported any explosions, sparks, or injuries suffered from the results of clicking any button or connecting any cable to a computer.

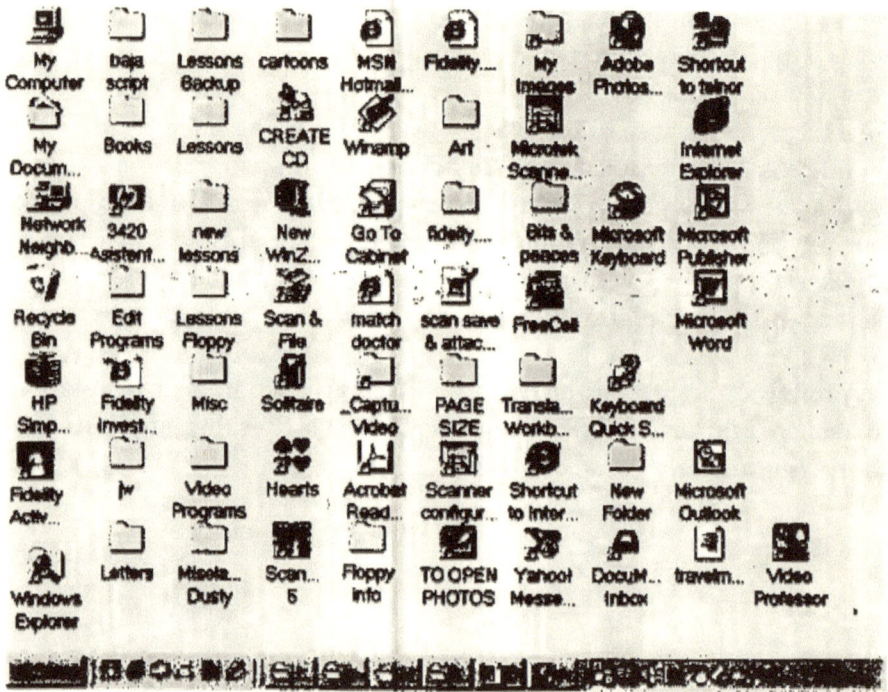

TASKBAR

The taskbar is on the very bottom of the monitor screen, with the Start button on the left side and your local time on the right end. In between, you will find an assortment of symbols, most of which are self-explanatory. Placing the arrow on each symbol can identify them.

There are operations you can perform without going online, and I will give you several at this time. You can write a letter on Microsoft Word, you can check folders and icons, and if you only have one telephone line in your location, working off-line will allow you to receive phone calls.

The picture above is a crowded desktop. In the beginning, you will have very few folders or icons. The calendar, clock, and several other toys to play with are on the taskbar,

MOUSE

The mouse can be considered your main control; it does so many things, or causes so many things to happen. The mouse got its name—you are right, it does look like a mouse. Most things change, and so has the little rodent, but regardless of the shape or size, they all operate the same way.

This little friend becomes active when you turn on the computer and your desktop appears on the screen. Also, the arrow, like a small relative of the mouse, could be hiding, so just slide the mouse around, and the arrow will show up.

When you are going over your lessons, you will receive instructions like, move the arrow, or take the arrow to this and that. Then you have left and right click—these are the buttons on the left and right side of the mouse. Your instructions will be to which side and how many clicks to cause the proper action.

OK, lets try it. On the desktop, move the arrow to My Computer and click twice. Good. Now go to Start and click one time. OK. Move the arrow to the top of the screen. Now let us assume that you had no mishap on the trip around the screen, so this being the case, practice for ten more minutes, and then you can consider yourself a mouse moving guru.

GOING ONLINE

Turn on the computer and wait for the desktop to appear. Then click twice on the Internet icon symbol, and after a bit, a page with msn and a small insert window, with a space for you to type in your e-mail address and password, will be waiting.

Sign in, and soon your e-mail page will appear, and in the center of the page, you will find the following:

    Mailbox usage
    My messages
    From My Contacts
    Junk e-mail folder

When you have time, go through this page very carefully, from the top line, the Hotmail icon, down next to the File bar (which you will use often). Many of the symbols will become apparent as you pass the arrow over them.

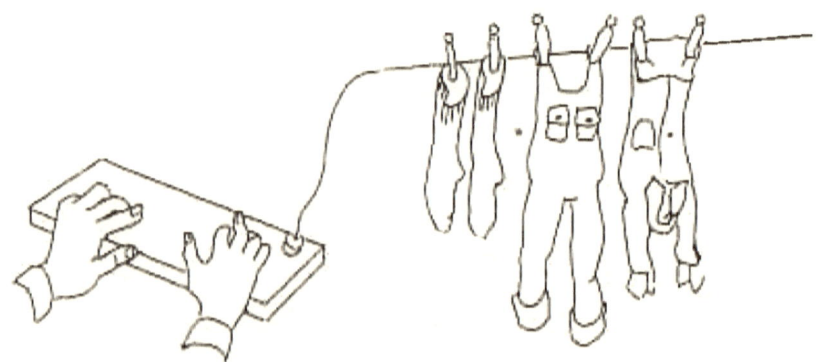

SENDING YOUR E-MAIL

On your e-mail window, you will see four buttons labeled Home, Inbox, Compose, Contacts. The last two, Compose and Contacts, are important to you for sending e-mail. Click on Compose if you have the address written down but not in your contacts or address book. The form for e-mail will come up, and you will fill in the blanks: the e-mail address of the person you intend to contact, the subject, and your message.

Contacts is your address book, where you will add information from time to time to use automatically for friends and/or businesses you want to contact often. You can enter their e-mail addresses by clicking on Compose, and then click the page for new contacts and fill in the form. Should you have an address for Tom, Dick, and Jane, and want to send each of them the same message, click on all their names on the contact list, and when you are ready, click Send, and your e-mail is on the way.

Now for a few rules of the game. In the beginning, read carefully all the windows or drop-downs, uninvited or not, and act accordingly. Next, always take the arrow to where you want to work. For example, when you have written your subject on the e-mail form and then to the space for your Dear John, you start to type and find your words are being added to your subject on the form above instead. Too bad. Start over, and this time, take the arrow to the flashing cursor to where you want to work first.

E-MAIL STEP-BY-STEP

To receive

1. Turn on the computer.
2. Wait for the desktop to come up.
3. Click on Internet icon.
4. When asked, type in your name and e-mail address.
5. If all is correct, take the arrow to Sign In.
6. Select the messages you want to read.
7. When finished click Back.

To send

1. Repeat steps 1 through 5.
2. Click New.
3. Click on Message.
4. Enter the e-mail address and type your letter.
5. Check the spelling and click on Send.

To spell correct

Go to Tools on the upper bar, and on the menu, select spell correct with a click.

Words misspelled will appear on your text with a colored underline. Correct spelling will appear with choices if the computer is in doubt as to that you want. You make the choice.

Should the word be spelled as you want it, press Ignore, and the computer will continue checking.

SAVING MESSAGES AND PRINTING E-MAIL

When you are on Hotmail, you have two options prior to sending the message. The first is called saving the draft. When you go to that option, you will save the message but not send it.

The second option is to save the outgoing messages. This option will let you save a copy of the message that you sent. In this order, you will first send it and then print the message.

When you have already saved the draft massage and you want to go back to it, just go to the Folders option on the Internet. Click to open it. You will find many options; choose the one that says Draft and click. When you open the folder, it will show you the many messages that you have recently saved. Click the one you want, and it will open on the screen.

If you have already sent it and you want to keep a copy, do the same process but instead of selecting Draft, take the outgoing messages option, and you will see a list of the messages that have been saved.

Now you can print it if you haven't already done so.

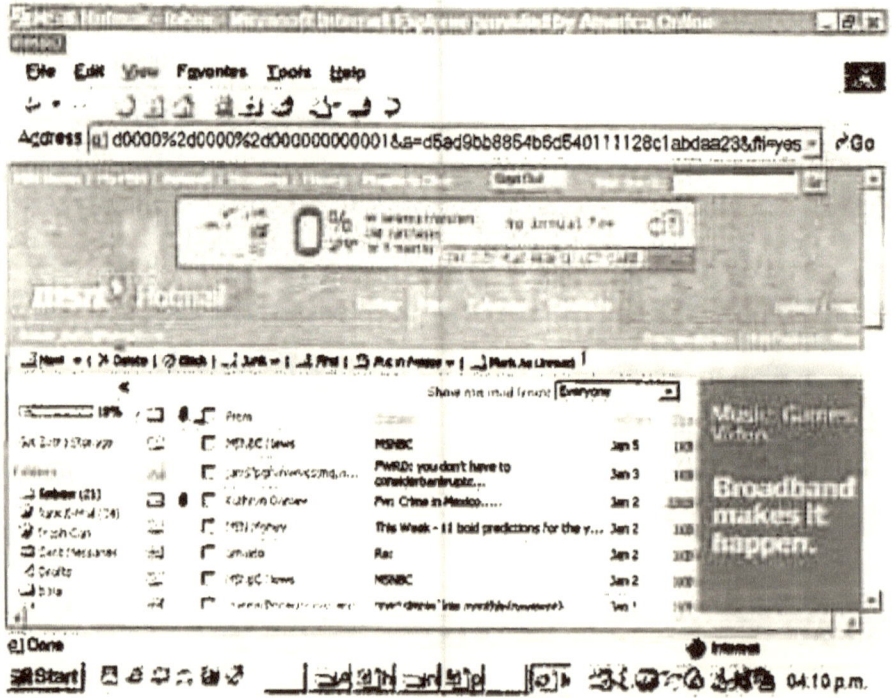

Having clicked on Mail on the previous page, you will see with the above page, which is your received e-mail.

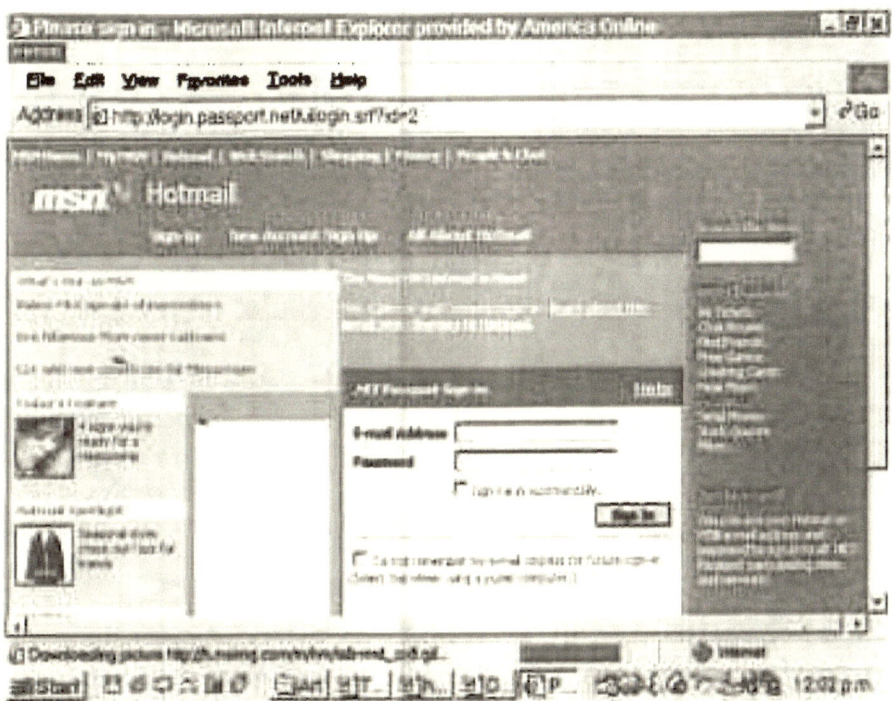

This is one of several ways to get to your incoming e-mail. Sign in with your address and password. Take a look at the gray bar on the right side; this will move your copy up and down.

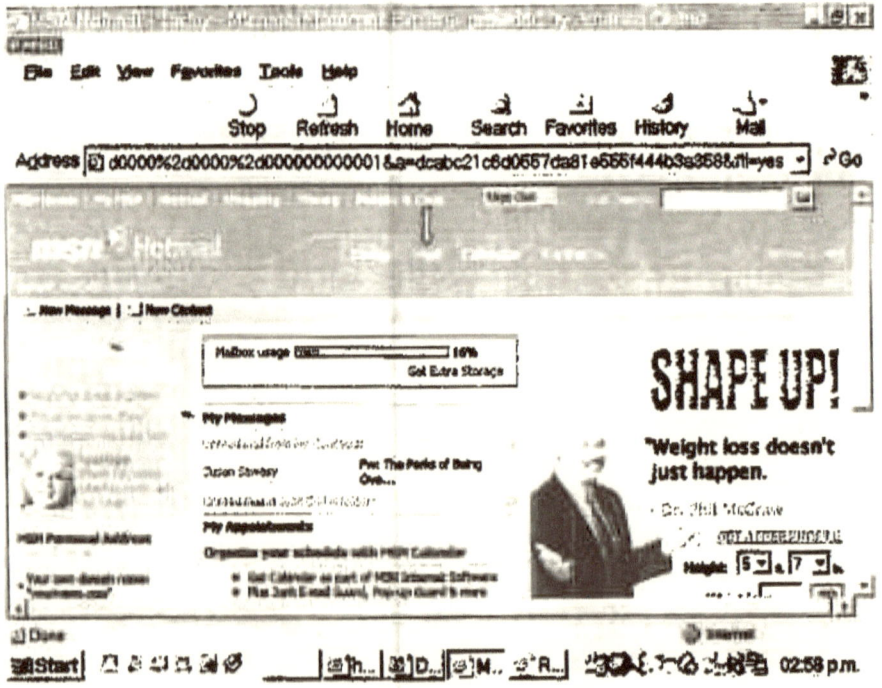

This follows after you have given your password and clicked on Mail. It will bring up your e-mail. Please check the page carefully.

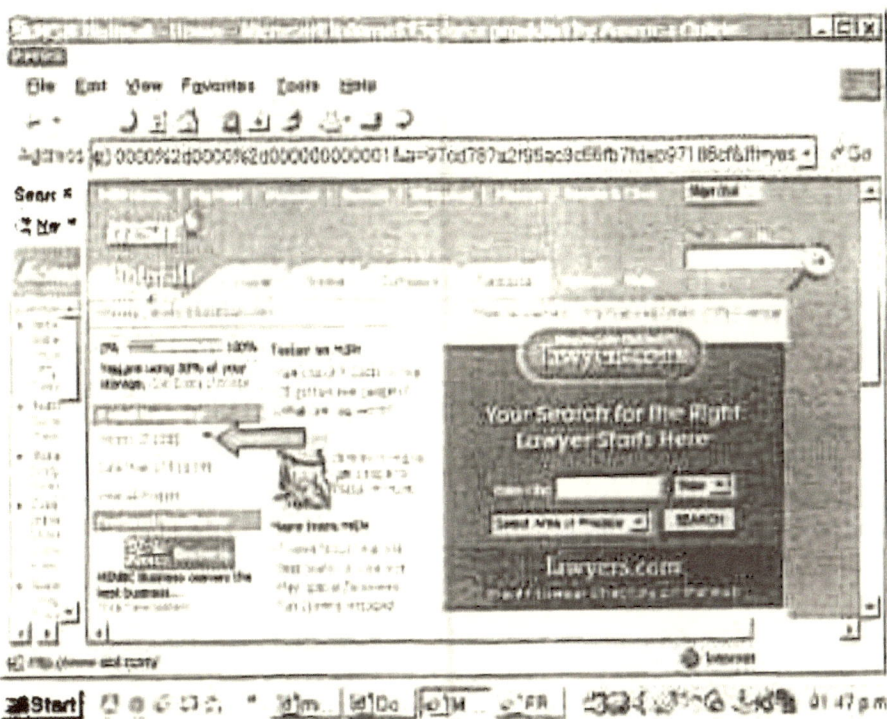

Please check the tabs in the solid blue in the box. They are Home, Inbox, Compose, and Contacts. Try out the gray bars on the side and bottom; they each have a small arrow to show you which way the copy will move.

ATTACHMENT

How to receive and bring it up to the screen.

ATTACHMENT: HOW TO RECEIVE

The incoming mail will tell you if there is an attachment in the blue area. Take the arrow to the Attachment button and left-click. Now wait for the clear sign, which is green check mark. Click on the Download File and open the file from its present position. Then you have to wait for a short time for the computer to return from is break.

SCANNING

Due to the numerous manufacturers of scanning equipment, it seems almost impossible to give you a detailed direction on your unit.

I advise you to pay close attention to the manufacturer's instructions. This should be on a floppy disk or a CD. And then follow the wizard's directions.

SCAN, SAVE, AND ATTACH

Go to the Internet, scan what you want to attach, and it will appear on the desktop. Now go to File and click on Save As and the Save icon appears automatically on the desktop line, go to the right and click on the second button.

From there, go to where it says File name, and if there is something written there, clear it by backspacing, and then type in the name you want for the file. In this case, it will be on the same line. Click on Save.

Then close the window with the X in the upper right-hand corner of the screen. And now you must bring up the e-mail page. Go to Compose on the e-mail page. Next, you will attach the file by going below the address line, where you will see the attachment space. Click on that and the attachment page appears.

You then click on Browse and choose File. A window will come up, check the first line of this file, and find looking in. Then you select where to put the file. This time we choose Desktop, but any file is fine. When we choose Desktop, the entire desktop will come up, and you can select the name you scanned.

When you have made your choice, you click on it once, and it will automatically come up on the file bar below. You can click Open, then again it will come to the attachment page (this is only on Hotmail). Then on the right-hand side, there is a little square window with an attachment button, and you click it, the file will go up to the attachment page. Then you wait.

The next window that comes up will be the same window already with the attachment. You will see it in the little square box, and it will have the name you gave it for file, then click OK. When you click OK, it will go to the Compose page, with the attachment in place and ready for you to fill in the name and e-mail address you want and any message you wish to add, and then you can send.

REMOVING UNWANTED E-MAIL

To delete any unwanted e-mail messages, go to the small box to the left of the sender's name and click once.

Then take the arrow to the bottom of the received e-mail, and you will see the box Delete. Click it, and the message is history.

Should you be ready to delete more than one message, use the procedure above. Do not stop with one; click on all the e-mails you want to remove.

GARBAGE REMOVAL

What I refer to as garbage is any copy you do not want to save from e-mail. Your friend, for example, has sent you a joke, and you would like to save it. However, your friend thought so much of the joke that it has been sent to over three hundred other friends. Now you have a joke, including the three hundred names. What to do?

Well, you really don't want to put your copier to all that work. You don't want to waste the time, and you might begin to wonder if the joke is really that funny. But fortunately, here is the solution:

1. Go with the arrow to the beginning of the copy you want to save. Hold the click down and highlight all the copy you want to save.
2. Take the arrow to File and select Print and click. Now look for the outlined word Select, and take the arrow to the Select spot.
3. Click OK.
4. Your copy comes on screen without the garbage.

PREPARING TO WRITE A LETTER

Reading time: 4 minutes
Execution: (with a little practice) 32 seconds

You will find that this is quite important as the basic procedure is involved with many other procedures that you will want to have available in your memory bank for important work and to enjoy working in this new field.

Go now to your desktop by turning on the computer and waiting for it to come up or take the arrow to either X or—, each are on the upper right-hand corner of the screen, press either, and the desktop will come up. Then proceed to select Microsoft Publisher or Word and click twice.

A Microsoft page with all the options will appear, forget them (for now) go to the bottom of the page to exit catalog on the lower right-hand corner, and click, and you now have a blank page. Go across this to the vertical bar on far left of the page and click on the A.

Move the arrow back to the page, click on the upper left corner while holding the click down to drag. A small cross will appear, and now, holding the click down, move the arrow to the lower right corner of the page and then release your finger, and the rectangular form will be evident. A form the gurus call a box, which will be the size of your letter page.

How do you suppose they can call a frame a box?

Should you prefer to use a smaller box rather than a full page, it is possible by holding the click and moving as you did before to the size of box you want with in the page size, and then release your finger.

Relax, we are almost there.

Take the arrow to the page and click it anywhere, and small black squares will come up at the corners and the middle of each border. This is your working frame. Take the arrow inside the box and click anywhere. Now look to the upper-left corner and behold. You will see a small flashing cursor, and it means you can type. However, you won't want to work in this small space, and a menu appears for you to make a selection of your choice or to make further adjustments. Go back to the second bar to the percentage box. Go to the right, to the plus or minus signs, and click your choice.

The page will be either enlarged or minimized. You will find a cursor waiting for you to start typing (not a serious letter like the one to Aunt Bertha), just a note so you will know this all works.

MAKING A LETTER ON MICROSOFT

In order to follow these instructions to the end, you must have a folder to file your work. If you have a folder you choose to use, good. If not, go to the table of contents for creating a folder. You are now ready to file.

Go to Microsoft Publisher on your desktop. Click twice, and a box or window with many programs will show. Go to Cancel. On the lower right-hand corner, click, it and a blank page will appear.

Now go to the left of the blank page, and click on A, which is nearly at the top of the vertical bar. Keep your clicking finger on the mouse and an X or cross will follow. Hold the click and drag the cross to the upper left-hand corner of the blank page, and from there, go diagonally down the page to the lower right-hand corner of the page and release your finger. The drag is complete, and you now have a frame. Take the arrow to the bottom of the bar, select Zoom, and click on 75%. This will enlarge the frame for easy typing within the blank square.

You are now ready to type. Start within the page at the top left near the flashing cursor. You can start anywhere, just put the cursor where you want to start, move it by using the four arrow-marked keys on the keyboard.

When your letter is finished, take the arrow to the left on the top bar to File. Click on this, and a submenu will appear.

Now with your hands on the keyboard, look to the right of your little finger, and you will see a cluster of four keys, each with an arrow pointing in four directions.

Then go back to your letter. You probably do not see the cursor. If you do, good. If not, take the arrow to any place within the text and click. Now you have the cursor and the four arrow keys to play with. Spend some time experimenting with them—you will learn more with playing than I can ever explain.

To enhance your fun and delight, I, at this point, highly recommend two things: one, a little refreshment, and then we will go to bar 3. This will help to make it all come together, and you will have some fun. The three bars are above, just under the bar with the percentages.

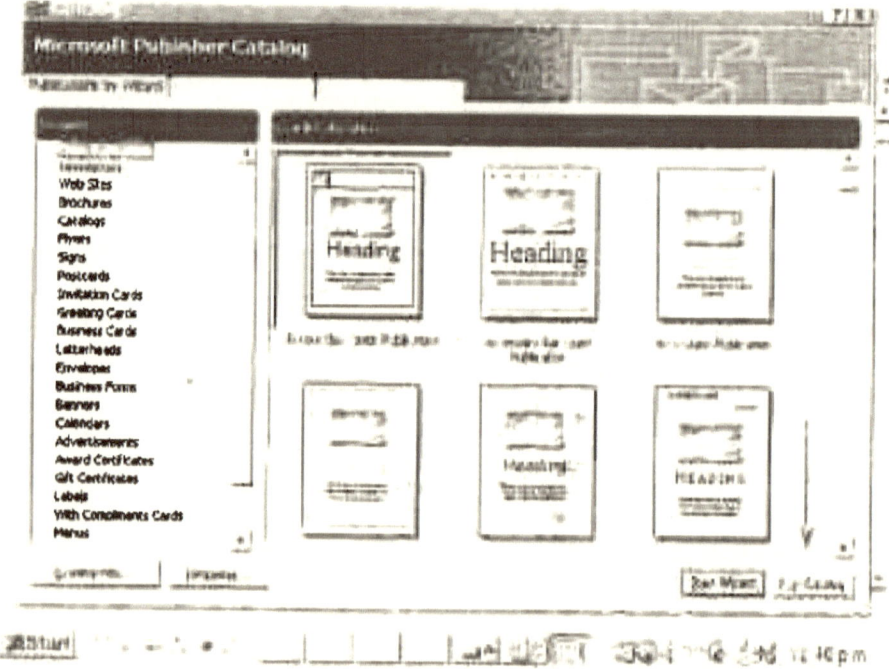

When on the desktop and press Microsoft Publisher this window comes up and you will click on Exit Catalog and follow our direction to prepare to write a letter using Microsoft Publisher.

WRITING A LETTER USING THE MICROSOFT WORD PROGRAM

To begin, you must have the Microsoft Word program installed or purchased with your computer, the same as Microsoft Publisher. Both will have an icon for your desktop.

Having cleared the hurdle above, turn on the computer and wait for the desktop to come up, then click twice on the Word icon and wait a very short time for a blank page with a flashing cursor. Start your letter at this point.

Let us take a look at the top of the screen, where there are several lines or bars. On the second line are small pictures and miscellaneous symbols. Please read on, and you will know all about this bar. We will skip the first place and go to the second, which is the choice for different types of fonts. By clicking the arrow, you will bring up a menu, and by moving the arrow through the selections, pick the one you prefer. Now on your own, you can go along this bar. Each image will be described. Please try all of them.

This is an example of what you might want to do. Let's say you want to put the word *example* in bold. OK, we take the arrow to B for bold, which is on top of the screen. Click it. Then place the arrow on the first letter on *example*, click, hold down, and drag the arrow across *example*. It will turn to white letters with black surrounding. Then return to Bold, click it, and behold—you have a boldfaced *example*.

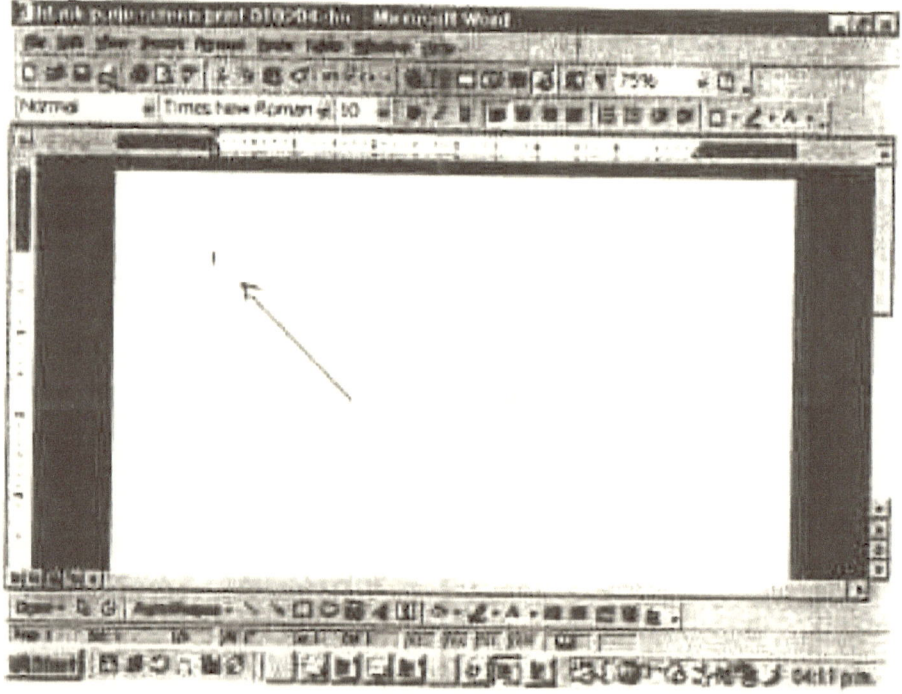

This is your beginning page when you have selected Word for typing your letter or other work. This comes up at once, and you will notice the cursor mark where you are to begin typing.

REDUCING PAGE SIZE

Begin on the desktop and click twice on Microsoft Publisher.

1. Bring up the blank page. For Microsoft
2. Go to File and click on Page Setup.
3. Go to Page Size, click on it, and fill in the size you require. Then click OK.
4. The blank page appears, and the arrow goes to A, then to the outside border and make your frame.
5. Now minimize.
6. Bring up your file, the one you want to minimize.
7. Highlight the text.
8. Press the right click and select Copy.
9. Minimize.
10. Click inside the frame.
11. Click the right button.
12. Select Paste, and you're finished.

ADJUSTING SPACE BETWEEN LINES AND CHARACTERS

Should you feel you want to change the space between lines you have typed, go to Microsoft Publisher and take the arrow to the top bar and click right on the Format menu. A small frame will appear with selections; take the one for line spacing.

Now a small box will appear, and you can select what is the best space for you by clicking the up and down arrows. You can also preview your style of type at this time.

The same process is used for the space between characters.

PRINTER

Time for this program with very little practice: three minutes.

There are several makes and designs of printers, and the best information I can give is when you have done some homework and chosen a printer, you should follow the directions carefully. There will be the usual dos and don'ts to follow to protect your warranty.

Most printers will have directions for cleaning and maintenance, so keep a schedule depending on the amount of work you do. This could be a good time to take the arrow to Start. Click it and directly above Start is a long vertical list of options. This time you select Settings and choose the name of your printer, then click right, then select Properties. Now click on Service, and the computer will do the rest.

There are two ways for you to know how to put the printer into action. First, on your monitor, you bring up what you want to print. This can be work you have just finished or any work you may have filed. Click twice on where you have your work in file; it will show on the screen. For work you have just finished, this is the time you should save it.

To save your work is very simple: leave your work as finished. Take the arrow to File and click it. This brings forth a menu, and you will find Save and Save As. You will select Save As, and the computer will put your work back.

No need for a great deal of memory work so far, right? But here comes the hard, tough part, so please pay close attention as there could be demerits should you fail. We started by having you type several lines on your page to get several lines for you to play with; a short note to a friend will do nicely. Now go to the left of the first line with the arrow, click, hold it down, and move the arrow from left to right and down through your prose to the end. You will notice a serious change: all is black. Now move your finger off the clicker.

Whoopee, time to take a breather. OK, now move the arrow to the third bar and go to Bold. Click it. OH BOY, look what happened to your friend's note! We must correct this. Take the arrow to the text anywhere and click; the black is gone, and the lettering is in bold. The tricky part is to remember that all the symbols on the third bar work the same way.

No need to black out the whole page—oh, I mean highlighted, as the gurus prefer, but as I was saying, you are not required to highlight the whole page. You can do a paragraph, a line, or just a word. Also, it is nice to know you can use all the third bar options at one time. Should you suddenly discover the third bar has gone someplace, not to worry, go with the arrow to your page, type a few characters, and the old third bar will come running right to where it belongs.

Now with your hands on the keyboard, look to the right of your little finger, and you will see a cluster of four keys, each with an arrow pointing in four directions.

Then go back to your letter. You probably do not see the cursor. If you do, good. If not, take the arrow to any place within the text and click. Now you have the cursor and the four arrow keys to play with. Spend some time experimenting with them—you will learn more with playing than I can ever explain.

To enhance your fun and delight, I, at this point, highly recommend two things: one, a little refreshment, and then we will go to bar 3. This will help to make it all come together, and you will have some fun. The three bars are above, just under the bar with the percentages.

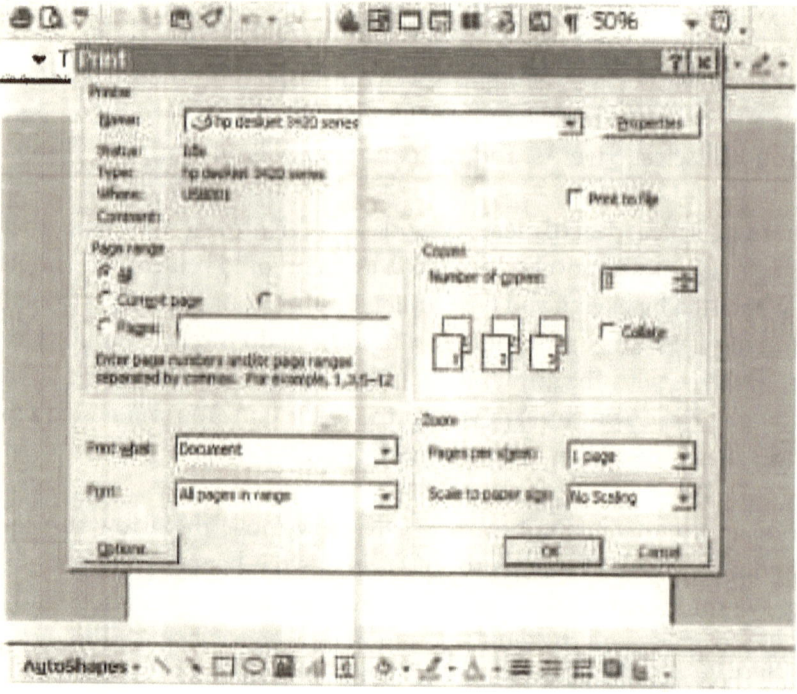

BAR 3

Bar 3 is the place to go for fonts, color styles, and all sorts of good things that will hold your interest, and think of all the possibilities. I will explain the procedures in this lesson with the hope that you will know that I have tried not to keep all the instructions for the subject on the same page. To do so in all cases has become a little redundant; therefore, I am asking you to commit a few applications to memory, and if you have to go back to the original instruction for a little reminder, turn to the table of contents for a quick refresher. You will find that in the future, the procedures will become automatic.

Let us talk about bar 3 on the Microsoft procedure. Hopefully, you have opened the program and the screen is in front of you. The bar will show you a strip of fifteen small pictures or symbols in the following numbered order: Number 1 will show you Style and is used for special projects. Number 2 shows Times New Roman (then click on the small arrow for more selections). Number 3 is font size (try 10 in the beginning). Number 4 is for boldface type. Number5 is for italics. Number 6, ABC, is for all characters to be in upper case. Number 7 has a small color square for adding color to your characters; click your choice. The next four pictures are for your selection of how you want the borders of your copy to appear—normal, type-centered, right side justified, or both sides justified. The following icon, number 12, is attention marks or numbering. Number 13 is for putting color in the background. Number 14 is for borders or framing. And number 15 is for deleting or adding shadows.

When you have time, go back over the options for use in the future.

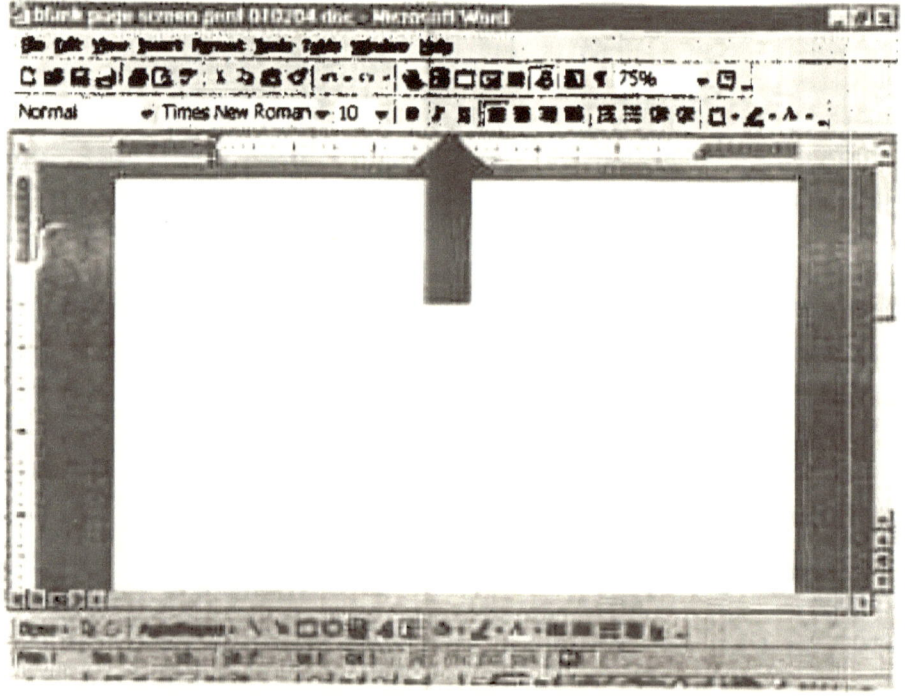

The arrow is to show you the third bar, which you will
use a great deal as indicated in your directions.

HOW TO DRAG

I will give you instructions as simple and as uncomplicated as I know how, by using the process of setting up to write a letter. Carefully follow the directions.

By turning on the computer and pausing, the desktop will come up. Move the arrow to the Microsoft Publisher icon, click twice. Now on the first page, click on the word Cancel, at or near the bottom of the page. A blank page will appear. Now take the arrow across the page to the vertical bar on the left side of the screen to the letter *A*. Click it and take the arrow to the upper left-hand corner of the blank page. Click there, but continue to hold your clicking finger down. A small cross will show up, and you will move the arrow diagonally down the page to the lower right-hand corner. You will notice as you move the arrow down, with your finger still on hold, that a black line is following the arrow. When you carefully reach the corner, you can remove you finger. And you have formed a box or frame and completed a drag.

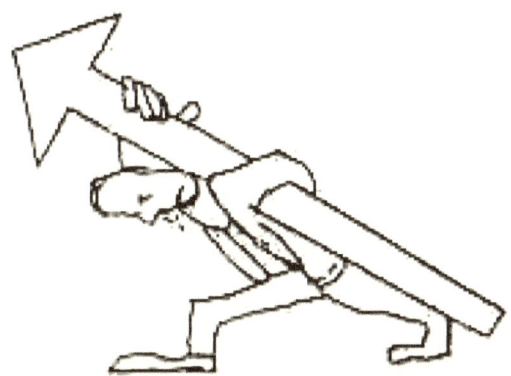

Should you feel it might be a good idea to make a copy of the text between the two lines and paste it on your tower or some place handy, so that when you are proceeding through the computer jungle with a tribe of gurus after you, you won't have to waste time then to find the How To for a drag. You will not have to leave it stuck up wherever very long for in a few practice periods, you will have it down pat. I will wait until you have used the drag to move a window, move some icons around, or perhaps do a layout, before presenting you with the official dragster cap.

TO MOVE A WINDOW

Move the arrow to the edge of the window you wish to move. When the double-pointed arrow appears on the line, click and keep your finger down (drag position). Continue to hold your finger on the click. You can then move the window to where you want it to go.

Should you lose contact with the line, click again and once more go to the window edge and go ahead with your move; you have done nothing wrong. Practice will help.

In the event that you cannot see the edge of your intended move, try reducing your image size by clicking Restore, the middle button next to the X on the upper right of the big screen.

When changing the size or position of a second window in your layout, please remember the window in blue is the one you are working; the gray one will not respond.

DOING A LAYOUT FOR A BROCHURE

Go to Microsoft Publisher on the desktop and click twice. We will use the same process to get a blank page by going to the exit catalog on the page with all the options. Exit is on the lower right corner. Click it, and you have a blank page. To make it a size reasonable to work with, press the small arrow on the right of the Zoom options on the second bar and select 30%.

Now go to File on the first bar and look for Page Setup and click once. At the bottom of the page, you will find a choice of Portrait or Landscape. We select Landscape and click it. The page is now in the horizontal position.

The next step is to arrange for the layout on the page and we go to Arrange on the upper bar and click once, and then again on Layout Guide. We click on it, and a small window appears on the screen.

The screen tells you that the margin guides have to be one inch from each side. When you have all of this taken care of, continue on to the next very small windows, and their heading is Grid Guide. You can select as many columns or rows that you choose. If you choose three columns, OK, and should there be a number in the choice square, just backspace it out and type in *3*.

HOW TO MAKE A BROCHURE

Go to your Microsoft Publisher and click twice. The screen that appears gives you the option of doing any kind of document, business card, letterhead, signs, etc. Choose Brochure using the arrow, and click OK. It will then introduce you to the wizard, which will take you step-by-step and show you the many options available. Select what you prefer and click on the image.

On the bottom right, you will find Next. Click it. Watch for this on each page through the wizard's assistance.

DISPLAY PROPERTIES

Possibly, this procedure could be better named. Perhaps *playground* would be more descriptive. Whatever!

Now let us go to the desktop and pick a blank space and click right. A menu will drop down, and you will select Properties, and from this point on, it is playtime. You will see buttons called Tags and other choice buttons. Take your time, click all of them—one at a time of course.

During this playtime, you will find it interesting to know that almost any item filed in your computer can be brought forward to enhance the screen like a personal or scenic photograph.

The message and the instruction is as follows: have fun in the display properties program. You will go back to it time and time again. Let your imagination take its course.

MAKING A BUSINESS CARD

On the Microsoft Publisher, and click twice. The first box with many selections will appear. Go directly to Catalog, at the bottom of the page on the right, and click twice. A blank page will appear.

Take the arrow to the first bar and in the upper left to File. Click it, and a menu will come up. Select Page Setup. Click it, and it will give you the four options: Normal, Special, Fold, and Special Size. On the lower box and on the small box, you will find a selection that is titled Publication Size.

Click on the small arrow, and you will find Business Card size. Click it. Take the arrow to OK, click it, and you have an enlarged standard-sized card in order to make it more convenient for typing.

Now is the time to experiment. Go to the vertical bar near the top, where you will find Font Schemes. Click it, and take the arrow to the upper left corner of the card, click it, and hold your finger down. A small cross will appear. Keep your finger down on the click, and then you can move the arrow to the form or draw a box. In this case, it could be for the name.

Having drawn in the size and position you want, release your finger. You can then type in whatever should go in to the frame.

In the beginning, I suggest you rough out what you want and where you want it so you can better organize things on the card—type style, font—and when you are happy with your results, it is time to save and prepare to print it.

Now go to the upper bar, then to File. Click there and select Save As on the menu, and click again. A menu will appear with an option Save in. Click on the arrow, and still another menu arrives, and you will click on My Documents. After the click, put the name on the file name box and click Save.

You may feel more comfortable in the beginning to work with the wizard, or you might want to check back and forth to both if something is not quite clear. Either set of instructions will put a business card in your wallet or bag.

The following is an introduction to Mr. Wizard. Go to Microsoft Publisher, click twice, and the screen will give you a variety of options to choose almost any kind of document. Look them over.

Then choose Brochure by clicking on it, and as soon as you click OK, you will be introduced to Mr. Wizard, who will take you step-by-step and show you the many options that are available. Select what you like and click on it.

Now on the bottom right of each of the wizard's instruction you will see Next. Click it. Look for this button on each page for the wizard's assistance.

CHANGING THE NAMES ON FOLDERS AND DOCUMENTS

First, we open the folder and select the document.

Click on it, then click right. A submenu will appear, and if you look near the bottom, you will see Rename. Click it. Now you can move the arrow into the file's name space. Using the arrow, move it to the right of where you want to make your change. Now backspace until you have removed all that you want to change (note: when you are backspacing, be careful not to delete the last three digits or letters), When you hit the backspace key, should the whole title disappear, a small symbol will take the place. Just proceed to type over it with your change, and everything will be OK. And then hit the Enter key.

You must remember not to assign a name or number that is already assigned to the folder or file. If you do, the computer will let you know and give you a chance to correct the error. You may be charged ten demerits.

CHANGING NAMES OF FILES AND FOLDERS

Step by Step

1. Take the arrow to the name to change.
2. Click right, a menu appears. Click on Rename.
3. Take the arrow to where you want to change.
4. Click right and highlight the original and hit Delete.
5. Place the arrow to the left of the three code letters, including the period (.doc).
6. Now backspace all you want to remove.
7. Type in your change.

CUT, COPY, AND PASTE

This is one of the most useful tools in editing a document. To take all or part of a text is called cut or copy (your choice). To take part of a text and place it within another document is called pasting. This process will become quite easy.

First you must know what to select, either cut or copy. You are working with text that you want to move to part or section of document A to include or relocate within document B. When being asked to select between cut or copy, you must know that to save all of A intact, you must choose copy, if you choose cut, the original will be lost.

From document A, select the text that you need to transfer to document B. Put the cursor on the first part of what you want to cut or copy, then click and hold down the left button and drag it to where you want it to the end of what you want to include or cut. You will see the text highlighted. Then move your arrow anywhere into the highlighted text, and click with the right button once.

Now a new small menu will appear. You will then be able to see the options: Cut, Copy, or Paste. Select Cut or Copy and click once. Now you have your text ready for pasting to the other document. Go to minimize at the upper right-hand corner of A or B. Document A is still available and waiting for a call. If you are doing this on the same document, you can skip minimizing.

To paste what you have ready, go to the place in the new document, or document B. Place the arrow where you want the copy to start, click again with the right button, and again, you will see the small menu. Select Paste, and you are now a cut, copy, paste guru.

Here is a short help menu for cut or copy and paste.

1. Bring up the copy A. Keep in mind the space. You want to include copy.
2. Bring up copy B.
3. Highlight the copy you want to move.
4. Click within the highlight.
5. Minimize A.
6. And B returns to the screen.
7. Place cursor where the paste is to begin.
8. Click with the right button and select Paste.

During this procedure, you will notice the lower bar (taskbar), where you will see both A and B, and this can be used to bring either to the screen.

Asterisk on 2, 5, and 6 no need to minimize if you are working on the same page. Please see first page of cut, copy, and paste.

CHATTING CAN BE FUN

There have been many chat lines from around the second year the telephone went into effect; they were called party lines on the telephone. Too bad today's gurus can't remember or haven't read a little history.

With chatting, there are possible advantages and disadvantages. With e-mail, you will always be waiting for a response. Chatting is quicker since you are typing messages to people right now; of course, they may not have the information you want. Now if you do not count the cost of the computer, chatting is less money than the phone. Then too, you may not care to whom you are chatting.

There are all kinds of abbreviations to use while chatting. I can give you a few, but it really goes on and on until you have played with it a little, but you can ask questions and type out what you want to say.

With regard to etiquette, you should, on a chat line, realize that you never know to whom you are typing a message and who is reading. Just be nice, stay cool, and if things get out of hand, shut down and go to a movie or phone a friend. Pretend you have been invited to a party, pay attention, find out what is going on. The slang use is something you will have to get used to.

I will supply you with a few abbreviations, but frankly, I prefer to call a Cadillac a Cadillac, not a cad, but that is up to you.

Be prepared to join a chat room and have a nice, name that's easy to remember. You can start on Yahoo! (http://www.yahoo.com), then check one, and one will lead to another. Check through the Internet and think about World Wide Web and Internet Relay Chat. There is information through your server, ask about Microsoft Chat.

Hear are a few abbreviations: *bbl*, be back later; *later mat*, great minds think alike; *j/k*, just kidding; *lol*, laughing out loud; *No*, no problem; *wtg*, way to go.

There are all kinds of precautions for us while chatting, but in most cases, common sense will see you through. Remember that all you read when chatting is not always true. A fellow chatter may be asking something that is none of his business. There are obvious things that you do not type—passwords, real names, addresses, etc.

As your chatting evolves, and if you have a good chatting service like AOL (America Online), you can set up your own chat room and let folks know what you want to chat about.

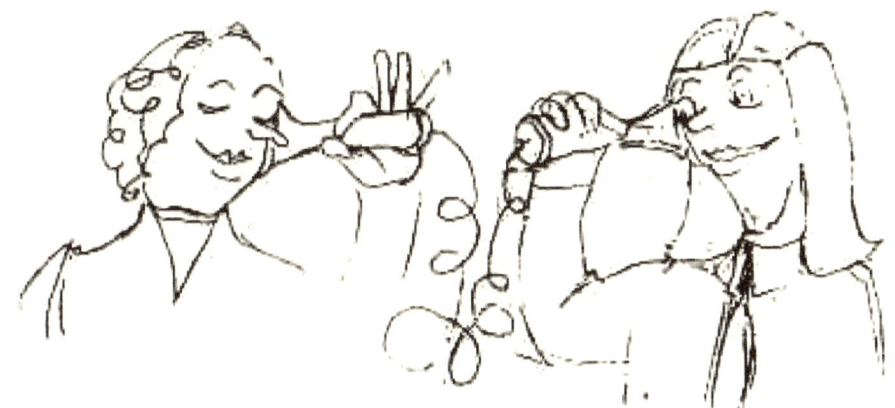

FINDING LOST FILES

A. Click Start.
B. Go to Programs.
C. Click on Windows Explorer, find your folder. Default folder is My Documents.
D. Click and look for original file.

Lost files
Search the file.
Click the program Windows Explorer.
Click on the left side.
Click on the first part of path C.
Click on My Documents folder, the second of path, folder.
Another list appears, click on the third folder if this exists.
If this is not the case, just look on the right-side list for your file.

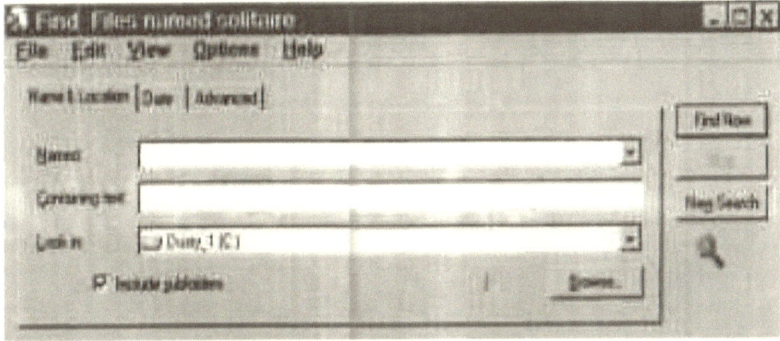

This can possibly give you a little extra help, and when you can ask for any and all assistance possible—find now, new search, check your spelling, and try again.

THIS PROCEDURE SHOULD HELP

Go to Start, and on the vertical menu above on the vertical list, look to find Files and Folders. Click on this to find all windows appear. Type in the name of the file you are looking for; be sure the name is spelled correctly.

Bringing up selected addresses.

First we want to bring up the address bar. One way is to click on Internet Explorer or when you go for your e-mail.

If you have the name and address, type it in and press Enter and wait a bit. If you do not have the complete address, you might want to guess, like the name of a well-known company. For example, type *www.newsweek.com*, then press Enter.

SURFING THE NET

Click on the Internet icon and go to the address bar. There will be something going on there. Just backspace it out, and for an example, let's use *www. newsweek.com*. You will type it in all lowercase as you see here. Then go to the right end of the address bar and click on Go Now. Wait a short time, and your request will come up, or you will receive directions or suggestions.

FORMATTING A FLOPPY

Should you require a floppy, it is best to buy them preformatted. However, this is how you can format a floppy, if it is required. Insert the floppy into the slot in the tower, which is A, then a drop-down menu shows up, and you will choose Format.

Click on your requirement, press Start. The computer will do more magic, and you will have a formatted floppy.

FILING WORK ON A FLOPPY

Bring the material you want to the main screen. Now place the floppy in the slot in the tower and take the arrow to File on the top bar, and then on the menu, click on Saves As.

The window Save As appears. On this window, you will see the name of your file in a small window, which is encouraging. Next, take the arrow up close to the Save As blue bar, and you will find Save in. Click it. Here on the new menu, you will find a small icon called Floppy 3 ½. Select this.

Now go back to the Save As window and find Save, and click it. A small hourglass will appear, and you will wait for it to stop rotating. When it stops, the window goes away, and your saved material is on the screen to do with what you will. GOOD SHOW

SAVING DOCUMENTS ON A FLOPPY.

1. Bring the copy you want to save to the screen.
2. Review what you want to save.
3. Go to File and click.
4. Select Save As.
5. Insert the floppy into the tower.
6. On the tab Save in, click on the little arrow. Then take cursor to 3 1/2 floppy and click.
7. Click on Save.
8. Careful, now close the document.
9. Only now do you recover and title the floppy.

HOW TO FILE AND RECOVER FROM A FLOPPY

The title indicates that you have something you want to save. This lesson will cover your requirements. You will think of all kinds of things to file for your convenience, and if you change your mind, there is always the recycle bin.

A. How to file copy on a floppy

Place the floppy in the slot in the tower and bring your copy to the monitor screen. To file, go to File on the first bar, click once, and from the menu, select Save As and click it. A box will appear asking where and what the name of the file is.

First is, where do you want it filed? Click the small arrow on the Save As line. A menu with floppy 3 1/2 will appear. Take the arrow to floppy 3 1/2, click it, and wait for the little clock to stop. Then close the file.

B. How to retrieving saved work from the floppy

Take the arrow from the desktop and move it to My Computer and click twice. Check for the name you want in the selection list, click it twice, and your selection will turn up on the monitor. You are now ready for future work. Perhaps a little editing?

RETRIEVING SAVED WORK FROM THE FLOPPY

Take the arrow to the desktop and go with it to My Computer and click twice. A box will appear with many selections, choose floppy 3 1/2 and click twice. Check for the name you are looking for in the selection list and click twice, your selection will appear on the monitor.

You are now ready for future work.

RECOVERING FILED WORK ON A FLOPPY

1. Place the floppy in the slot.
2. Go to the desktop, select My Computer, and click twice.
3. A box will appear with many selections. Choose floppy 3 1/2. Click it twice.
4. Look for the name you want to find; it will show up in the selection list.
5. Click it twice, and it will show up on the monitor.

FORMATTING A DISK
(If you have a CD writer)

Insert the CD by opening the lower tray in the tower. Do this by pressing the blue button on the right up by the tray. Once the CD is in place, press the same blue button again.

The computer will read the CD and send you a box or window, and you will be asked what kind of a CD you wish to make.

This could be to create a data CD accessible to a drive letter, to create a CD for distribution for different types of computers, or a CD player for music, or copy from a CD to a CD.

Click on the first one. This will take you to a wizard for a how-to-do step-by-step.

If you want to know if the disk is formatted, put it in the CD writer, and the computer will tell you.

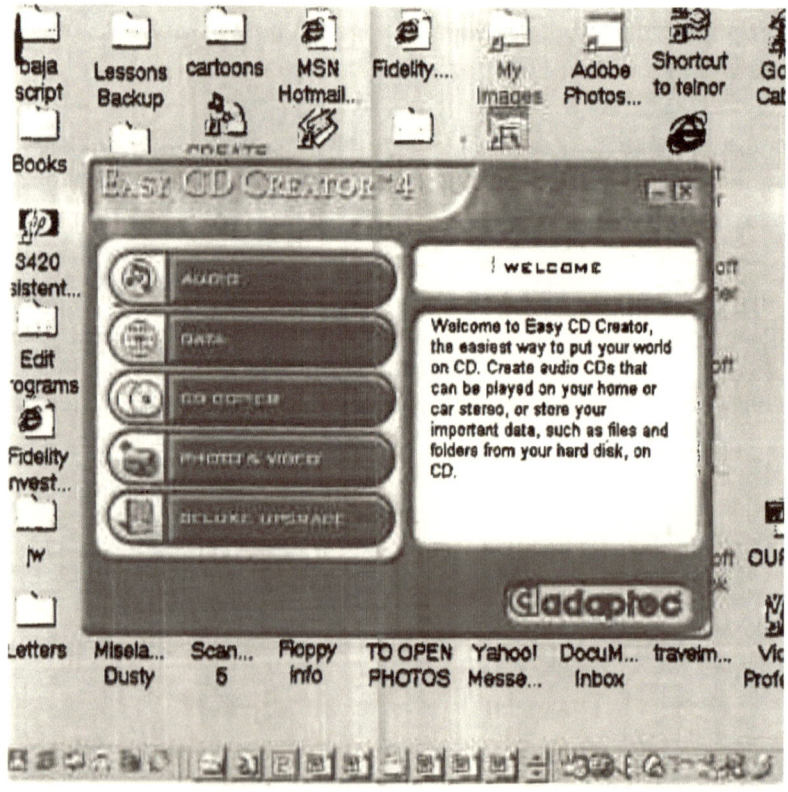

When preparing to work with CD-ROM or disks, you have to purchase the program Easy CD Creator 4. This will bring the program to the screen. Just follow the directions that come with the program.

RECORDING WORK ON A DISK
STEP-BY-STEP

Here comes a very nice bit of computer magic.

Let us talk about the disks. First they are plastic and, therefore, delicate. They come in a plastic case for protection, and they really shouldn't be taken out of their case until it is time to put them to work.

The disk should only be handled by the edge and placed in the tower carefully. The tray for the disk is easy to find—it is near the top of the tower with an opening button. Try it. If you have a CD writer (I will explain the writer later), that's about all the instruction you need regarding the disk. The step-by-step should clear it up for you.

1. From the desktop, click on the Create a CD icon (to be installed when required).
2. A window will appear called Easy CD Creator 4.
3. Click on the data tab.
4. Next comes the Creator.
5. Click on Next.
6. Look for the file or files you want to record, and click one.
7. Click Next.
8. Now click on Option (do not perform test).
10. Click on Next. And the click on Finish.
11. The program will tell you when it is finished.
12. When finished, the disk tray will pop out, and you now remove the disk. Close the tray and the program.

WHAT IS RECORDED ON A CD

Go to the My Computer icon and click twice. When the My Computer screen appears, you will see icons with letters of its drives.

Find the one for CD. Click twice, and a screen will open with nothing on it because as of now, we have nothing recorded.

When future recordings are made, you will see the entire file. Select the one you want to see and the one you want to take out. Click it.

At this time, you will be able to edit by the use of the Delete key. The Delete key is to the right of the large key.

Now you are ready to save on a disk. After you save on this, filing it could take up to five minutes. Watch the clock now, remove the disk, and label it.

You're finished, you did it, all is perfect. Please don't send for a refund.

RECYCLE BIN

Computers have the option to send the deleted files to a special icon or folder called the Recycle Bin. All computers have a recycle bin in case you make a mistake. So now, I have deleted a file by mistake, and I am going to bring it back to the same folder without losing it. This is very simple. I just go to the Recycle Bin, click it twice, and I will see the files I have deleted.

After you open the bin, you look for the file you deleted by mistake and click that file once with the left, and then click with right, and a menu will come up with only four options: Restore, Cut, Delete, and Properties. Click Restore and press Enter.

The computer will take the file and reinstall it to where it was. This is called magic in computer language.

EMPTYING THE TRASH CAN

Please be careful. This is a step up from the Recycle Bin, and this is permanent. Is emptying the bin what you want?

We proceed by clicking twice on the Recycle Bin. Up pops a few options. You will choose Emptying the Recycle Bin with a left click. Widows will nudge you again, asking if you are sure. If you say yes, all items in the trash can will go away. You will in turn free up space on your hard drive.

Should there be something you just can't part with, you can always make a copy on a floppy for insurance.

ADDING PROGRAMS

One of the most important procedures to eliminate problems with your computer is the correct installation of new programs and deletion of other programs; a software program is required and available at computer stores.

Proper deletion is accomplished by the above-mentioned Add/Remove Programs. Double-click this icon, and a window with several choices will appear, Install/Uninstall, Windows Page Setup, and Start Disk.

You should select Install/Uninstall by clicking on Word, which will give you instructions to install a new program using a CD-ROM or floppy, and when using this, look for the button Next and continue.

When buying a new computer, the company, at your request, will install any programs you desire and what they might recommend.

The computer needs information, and you should select the program you choose to remove, which is listed in Windows. If it is, click on it in order to highlight it. Click on the Add/ Remove button; this will ensure the program is removed with Windows' knowledge. A second method is to drag the unwanted program and any related folders to the Recycle Bin, but hold on to it for you may need to recall it should the computer behave other than normal.

GAMES

When buying a new computer, several games should be included. If special games are required, they must be purchased individually.

To open, perform the following:

1. Go to the Start button on the desktop and click.
2. Go up the vertical program to Games.
3. Cross to the right for games.
4. Then select the game you want.

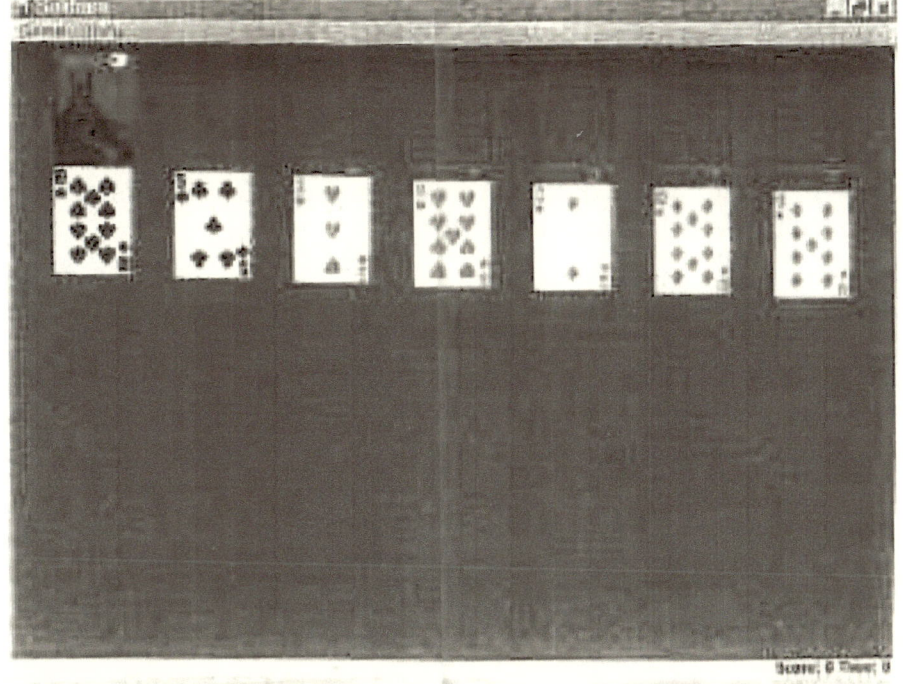

BITS AND PIECES

We have selected several questions that may come up or may need a little reminder and, in some cases, do not warrant major space in the workbook. Bits and pieces may save you a little time rather than going through a complete lesson.

Alt+F4 can be used to eliminate pop-up advertising of which you have no interest.

Arranging folders on the desktop, take the arrow to the open space on the desktop and click right. A menu appears, and you will select Arrange Icons, then select By Name.

Bringing up the third bar, go to the gray portion of the number 1 bar on the top of the monitor and click right. A small menu appears. Select Formatting, and the third bar will come up. Now drag it into position on the third line.

Browsing, do you have to be online to use it? Yes.

Computer freezes—this means things look normal but nothing works. In this case, press Ctrl+Alt+Delete at the same time. This will display a message indicating the frozen program or application.

Copy goes away. Copy that is in a file. Go back to the file, and click twice.

Date, time, day. Go to Time on the taskbar and click twice. The clock, the timer, and the calendar will appear. Use the arrow to make corrections.

Deleting a file. Click on the file only once and click Delete.

Enlarging small lettering. Take the arrow to the Zoom button on the third bar and select 75%.

Deleting copy or other material. Go to the first part of the text you want to delete, click and hold for a drag until you get to the last part that you want to delete. Now release the drag and press the Delete key.

Extremely small lettering, making it impossible to read. Take the arrow to the third bar to the Zoom button, click on the small arrow and select 75%.

Favorites, adding to: Select what you want to add, then go to Favorites. Then type in the name or description you want to save and click OK.

Filed work. When bringing up filed work and the computer tells you the file is being used, go to the taskbar, click on your file, and click on X.

Frame. Occasionally, you will start to file, and the computer will say, Oh no, you don't have to have a frame to type. OK, just go into the page with the arrow, click it, and behold, you now have a frame.

Getting back to the desktop. Click on the minus sign (upper right in the screen).

Going off-line. Using the little computers is the way to do it, but to get back online, you must go back to the desktop and start over.

Lost copy, should your copy in file go away. To get the copy back to the screen, go back to the desktop and double-click the folder and off you go.

Lost cursor. Take the arrow to your copy and click.

Lost address line. Take the arrow to Tools on the top bar and select Addresses, and it will appear on the fourth line.

Lost bar. To find a lost bar, go to the top one on the screen and click on Tools. A choice would be given, take your pick.

My Computer is your storage for your floppy disks.

Online. When I'm online how do I get off? Go to the little computer symbols on the task or lower bar and click twice.

Printing your e-mail. Type your message and take the arrow to dive, which is just above subject or below the address you are sending the e-mail. Now type in your own address, and now send your message, and your copy goes to your inbox so you can file or print.

Safe mode. The computer lets you know when it is operating in safe mode. Go to F8, and then, using the four directional keys, take the arrow to normal on an upper bar, then press Enter on the keyboard.

Second page. Should you find your typing will run over to the second page, go to the line above the taskbar. You will see page 1 with arrows on each side. Click the right arrow, and it takes you to page 2 when you need it, or on to page 3. You can return at any time.

Shutting down. You do this by going to the desktop and down to Start. Click it, and just above Start is Shut Down. Click it. Then a small window appears with options for you to choose.

DISCLOSURE

Regardless of how hard I try to balance a lesson between the young and the adult, there is always the chance I may talk down or up to the student. I try not to do either.

When presenting a lesson, there is always the chance that someone will want to show you a different way. Well, believe me, in the computer world, there are many ways to work a program. I have tried to keep things as simple as possible, leaving most shortcuts and tricks for the future. Hopefully, keeping it simple in the beginning will work best for you.

There are a lot of equipment, and I cannot be as exact in how to direct you. For example, you may have a scanner that I have never heard of. In a case like this, if you are buying used or new, always try to get the manufacturer's information disk or booklet. This includes new equipment you may purchase regarding the boxes the equipment has come in on, what should be there is there.

When starting something anew, I prefer to dip a toe rather than make a big splash in the computer pond. The splash may depend on your allowance or how the market has been treating you. Please keep in mind that computers are rather short-lived and the super gurus are making changes and creating new things that we are all expected to purchase as soon as possible, but there are a lot of new things that are not always required. Buy basic, like this book, and put it to work.

Should you become the owner of this effort to help you enjoy a computer, the following will be important to you. You will have questions as time goes by, and they can be handled in the following manner.

You may reach me by telephone, e-mail or fax.

If I do not have the answer to your question, I will know how to get the answer or solution you need, and it will be sent to you as soon as possible by the best way you will suggest.

Phone or fax: 920-344-2121
E-mail: *rhoads_dusty@hotmail.com*

INDEX